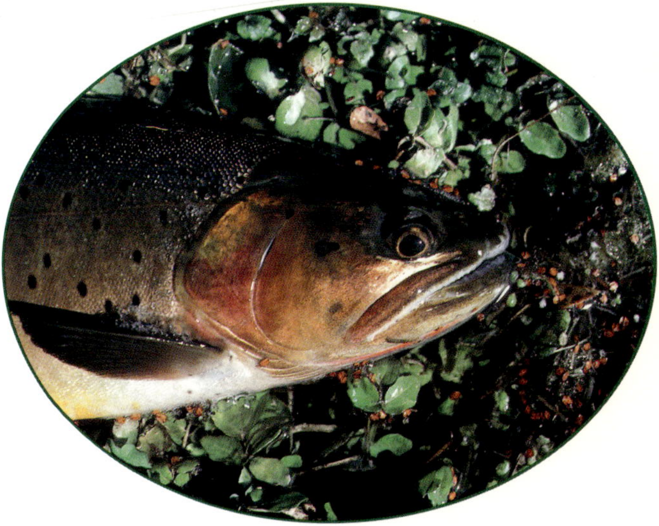

Harry Murray

Illustrations by Dürten Kampmann

Frank Amato
PORTLAND

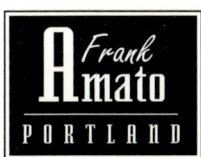

Acknowledgements

I am deeply indebted to the many people who have helped tremendously in the preparation of this book. Without assistance it could not be written. They are alphabetically: Bill Burslem, William Downey, Jack McAllister, Glenn Morrison, Jeff Murray, Dick Rabun, Gerald Racey, Cindy Simmons, Rhonda Tamkin, and Charley Waterman.

Dedication

This book is dedicated to my children:
Milly, Nicki, Liz, Jeff and Susan.

Other books by the author

Trout Fishing In The Shenandoah National Park
Fly-fishing For Smallmouth Bass
His Blessing Through Angling
Virginia Blue-Ribbon Streams

© 2003 Harry Murray
ALL RIGHTS RESERVED. No part of this book may be reproduced in any means (printed or electronic) without the written consent of the publisher, except in the case of brief excerpts in critical reviews and articles.

Photography: Harry Murray
Design: Jerry Hutchinson

Softbound ISBN: 1-57188-281-2
Softbound UPC: 0-81127-00100-2

Frank Amato Publications, Inc.
P.O. Box 82112, Portland, Oregon 97282
(503) 653-8108
Printed in Singapore
1 3 5 7 9 10 8 6 4 2

Foreword 6

Introduction 7

Chapter 1 8
TROUT AND STREAMS

Chapter 2 12
FLY TACKLE

Chapter 3 29
FLY CASTING

Chapter 4 33
NATURAL TROUT FOODS

Chapter 5 43
READING THE WATER

Chapter 6 55
SPOTTING TROUT

Chapter 7 71
EARLY-SEASON TACTICS

Chapter 8 80
LATE-SPRING AND SUMMER TACTICS

Chapter 9 98
THE FABULOUS FALL

Index 103

Foreword

I have known Harry for many years and have read his books and many of his writings. As with all his other endeavors in the sport of fly-fishing Harry freely shares his knowledge of the sport. Any angler seeking information that will improve their success while seeking trout in streams should benefit from this book. The information from *Trout Stream Fly-Fishing* is packed with answers that are often asked by many trout anglers. Harry will take you from your hat to your boots and all the necessities in between that are necessary in preparation for trout stream fly-fishing. His lifelong experiences of the many mountain streams where he pursued his love for trout are compiled in this book. Harry doesn't miss a trick when it comes to reading a stream and locating prime holding areas that are favored by mountain stream trout. You will learn the tactics that are successful in encouraging wary trout to take your offering. This is a must book for anyone interested in building their knowledge and success in fly-fishing for stream trout.

—*Bob Clouser*

Introduction

You are standing beside a beautiful little mountain trout stream. As the last rays of sunlight dance off the silvery surface of the pool, a trout rises before you, delicately sipping in a natural insect drifting on the surface. Seconds later, it sucks another insect from the surface, and this time, you see the trout as it turns below the surface.

You are very excited by this beautiful display of one of Nature's most highly respected creatures at work. But more than this, you are personally challenged. You want to match your skills against the highly refined natural instincts of this trout. For that matter, you want to find other trout in other streams against which you can test your talents.

This is a very worthy quest because the gratification one receives from mastering these angling challenges are extremely rewarding. The purpose of this book is to enable you to refine your angling skills so you can enjoy fishing for trout throughout the country.

By investigating the demands of trout and their natural foods we'll see how we can select the best flies to use in various situations. Discussions about tackle and instructions in casting will show you how to select and use the proper fly tackle. You'll see how to read the water and spot the trout in the stream so your time on the stream becomes a very rewarding personal experience which will grow with each successive trip.

In order to refine your techniques, we'll start in the spring and fish our way through the whole season. We'll meet and master all of the conditions we confront from the high, cold streams in the spring to the low, clear streams late in the summer.

Basically, you'll learn to accurately evaluate all of the stream conditions from a trout's point of view. Yes, you'll learn to think like a trout.

TROUT AND STREAMS

Fishing for wild trout in cool, clear meandering streams in beautiful settings is one of the most exciting sports available. I know of no other fish which gives one such wonderful gratification when the challenges it affords are successfully mastered.

The best way to master trout fishing begins with gaining an understanding of just what trout require in order to sustain themselves.

Fortunately there is overlap concerning the requirements of different trout species in different types of streams in different parts of the country. From the brook trout in the small headwater brooks, to the rainbows in the racing large riffles, to the brown trout under the banks in the slow runs, to the cutthroat trout in the high meandering streams, the basic needs are much the same.

They all need food, cover and spawning area. They also need to be able to feed efficiently. That is, they need to gain more food value from what they eat than the energy they must expend to capture it. The degree to which we understand and master these axioms will determine the extent of our success.

Fortunately this quest for more knowledge about trout fishing gives one a great amount of pleasure. Especially when the result is catching a worthy trout.

The late master angler Ed Hewitt ventured that the development of an angler usually takes a predictable course. When one begins trout fishing he wants to catch great numbers of trout, next he seeks the largest trout, and finally he's attracted to those trout which provide the greatest challenges. I fully agree with this

Headwater mountain trout streams are natural classrooms for the angler, each pool provides different challenges and rewards.

progression and feel that ultimately one experiences something deep and meaningful in the process.

STREAMS

I've always believed that the trout angler who wants to gain a solid understanding of the entire sport can do this best by starting on small headwater streams. In these streams which are less than 20 feet wide with pools only a little longer, everything is laid out before us in miniature. The demands are easier to evaluate here than on larger streams, and our successes or failures are more easily understood.

Each pool in a headwater stream is slightly different than the one above it and below it, and thus as one gradually fishes up the mountain the stream itself becomes the teacher. Learning how to approach each pool carefully, then evaluating the feeding areas, and finally making the presentation and catching the trout, assures you that you have done everything properly. Multiply this by many pools and many streams and you have a firm foundation of trout fishing experiences that you can confidently take with you as you fish the medium-size streams.

I consider medium-size streams as those which can reach nearly 100 feet wide and carry a much greater water volume than the headwater streams.

Many of the same tactics we use in the headwater streams are very effective here. But unlike the headwater streams which required that we use an upstream approach in order to avoid scaring the trout, we now have the option of using a downstream approach in many medium-size streams. My choice as to which approach to use on the medium-size streams is dependent upon the actual volume of the stream and the particular tactics I plan to use. If, for example, I believe there is enough water in the stream that my downstream approach will not scare the trout, I may decide to fish streamers which imitate the minnows in the stream. I will wade down the stream, and cast across and slightly downstream, and swim my flies across the current.

If I want to use dry flies or nymphs on the medium-size streams, I use an upstream approach because this enables me to present my flies to trout in a more natural manner.

The final type of stream we'll cover in this book is the high meadow stream. Actually, these may overlap with headwater and medium-size streams in size, but since we are often required to fine tune our tactics on these flat meandering streams I'll discuss these situations when we come to them so that you can effectively fish them.

Brook trout are native to the East where they still thrive in many mountain streams.

Chapter 2

FLY TACKLE

FLY RODS

The fly rod is usually the first piece of equipment that the new angler will purchase. In order to assure that this choice is made properly one needs to first determine the size of flies they will be using, for this governs the size of line that they will need. Once one knows the size of line that they will need, they can select the correct rod which will balance with the line. Simply stated, the fly size governs the line size and the line size governs the rod weight, but the length of the rod is governed by the closeness of the overhead canopy.

These three rods will cover all of your needs on small to medium-size streams. Top: 9 foot, 6 weight, 4 piece; 7 ½-foot, 3-or 4-weight, 4-piece; 6-foot 10-inch, 3-weight, 3-piece.

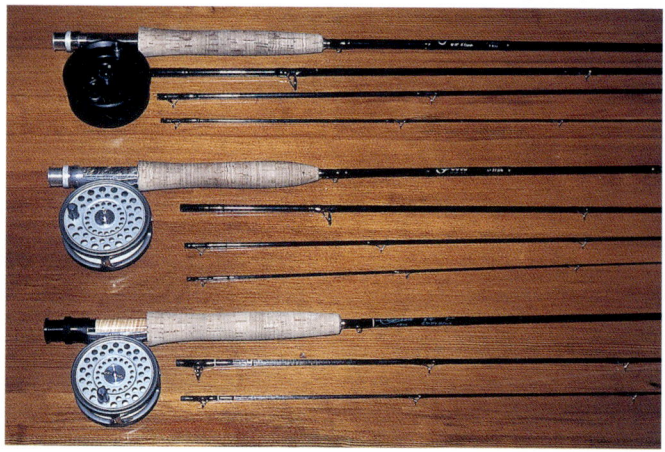

There is a large amount of small stream trout fishing in mountain regions throughout the country. We use flies ranging from size 12 down to size 22 on these streams and I like a size 3 line for these. The tree limbs often hang down close to the stream in these mountains and fly rods which range from six-and-a half to seven feet long will be best in order to prevent hitting the limbs when casting.

On slightly larger streams we often encounter greater water volumes and deeper pools, so we may use flies from a size 8 down to a size 22. Here, a size 4 line is ideal. Rods which range from seven-and-a-half to eight feet long are good here.

Medium-size trout streams (reaching up to 100-feet wide) often call for nymphs and streamers as large as a size 6 in the spring while we may slip down to flies as small as a size 18 during the summer. I like a size 6 line in these situations. And since overhead canopy is not a problem, I prefer a nine-foot rod because it helps me control the drift of my flies better than shorter rods.

FLY REELS

Reels for this type of trout fishing should be durable, with a light starting drag, and they should hold the line as well as about 50 yards of backing. Those for the three- and four-weight lines should weigh from three to four ounces. Reels for six-weight line should weigh from three-and-three-quarters of an ounce to five ounces.

FLY LINES

Floating fly lines cover the majority of needs that you will have on these streams. One style is the double-tapered line which is constructed with equal tapers on each end. They present the fly delicately, mend well, and give one the economy of being able to reverse the line on the reel when the front taper wears out. The second style is the weight-forward taper, which also permits delicate presentations, and enables one to easily shoot out longer casts when needed. The third style is referred to as a level line. These do not present the fly as delicately as the first two and do not cast as far as the weight forward. Yet, people often purchase level lines simply because they are less expensive.

When fishing streams that are approaching 100 feet wide, and which are carrying a full flow in the spring, one may find the moderately-fast sink-tip fly line useful when fishing streamers. These are weight-forward lines in which the first eight to ten feet of the line sinks at a rate of two-and-a-half to four inches per second. A nice feature of these lines is that they are fished the same way floating lines are, but these place the fly deeper in the water.

BACKING

A Dacron line of 20-pound test is used for the backing behind the fly line. This enables larger trout to run considerable distances, while still being under the control of an angler, and it helps to fill the reel, giving one a greater recovery rate when cranking in a trout than would be possible without backing.

LEADERS

Tapered leaders which are from seven to nine feet long—tapering down to 4X, 5X, 6X, and 7X—cover most floating line needs. (I like to use six-foot leaders tapered down to 3X or 4X with the sink-tip lines.)

VEST

A good fishing vest is a great help when fly-fishing. More expensive vests are usually more durable than economy models, and their pocket layout is usually more workable. But no matter what, always be sure that the model you purchase will hold the style and number of boxes that you use, as well as all of the other gadgets you use. In addition, I prefer vests which have large rear pockets that will hold raincoats. This can be very useful at times.

There are many chest packs which can be used to carry tackle too. These are lighter than vests, but most lack the greater capacity most good vests offer, and they also seldom provide the room needed to store a raincoat.

RAINCOATS

Raincoats are essential, and those made of breathable, waterproof materials are well worth the extra cost. Be sure your raincoat comes down over your waders or hip boots. I've used coats when wearing hip boots which did not reach over the boots and they acted like funnels running the water down my legs and into my boots. Raincoats should be large enough to wear over your fishing vest and the bulkiest jacket you ever plan to wear fishing.

WADERS

There are many types of wading gear for anglers. The first thing one needs to determine is the proper length for your personal needs. If you fish deep streams, the chest-high style will be best. If you do not want the bulk these have, you may prefer the waist-high style. If all of your fishing is done on small shallow streams, hip boots will be fine. If you fish only in the warm part of the season and need to walk very far to get to your stream, simple wading shoes may cover your needs.

Next, you can choose between boot-foot waders which are constructed all in one piece, or stocking-foot waders which are worn with separate wading shoes. Both of these come in various lengths and hip lengths.

Felt-soled wading shoes, felt-soled hip boots, neoprene waders and breathable waders are all popular with anglers.

Materials used to make waders may be neoprene, which is good in very cold water, breathable waterproof material, which is very comfortable, or lightweight waterproof coated nylon, which is very economical.

Wading shoes, which are used with stocking-foot waders in cold water, or alone in warm water, are constructed with canvas, synthetics and leather. When choosing a pair, select shoes that give the best support and protection.

Soles on wading gear may be constructed from rubber, felt, or felt with metal studs. I prefer felt on small streams and felt with metal studs on larger streams.

HATS

I believe a good hat or cap is important, but the underside of the bill should be a dark color to aid in seeing trout in the stream and to help your vision as you look into the stream to evaluate the various areas of cover for trout. I like dark or neutral colors that are not easy for trout to see in small streams. Hats should also be constructed with waterproofed or water-shedding breathable materials.

SUNGLASSES

Polarized sunglasses are essential to help you see clearly through the glare on the surface of the streams. This enables you to evaluate the stream bottom in order to determine where the trout will feed and to help you actually see the trout.

FLY BOXES

Fly boxes should have the capacity to hold all of the flies needed on a stream, and should be able to fit easily into the various pockets of a fishing vest. There are many excellent boxes made of various materials with many different methods of holding flies. I especially like those made of soft plastic with metal hinges which range from 1/2 inch to one inch deep.

GADGETS

There are many small tools and gadgets which anglers use that make various tasks easier and more efficient. Here are some which are very helpful.

Knot-tying tools are helpful for those just learning to fish. These should aid in tying the flies onto the leaders, adding tippets to the leaders, and attaching the leaders to the fly line. (See the instructions for tying these knots at the end of this chapter.)

Hook-sharpening files or stones are a must for keeping hook points sharp while we are fishing and should be used regularly.

Small leader clippers or scissors are needed to cut leaders and fly lines. Attaching these and many other small tools to the

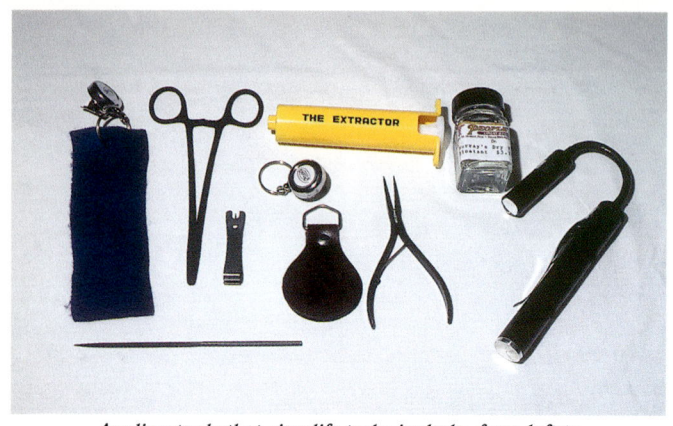

Angling tools that simplify tasks include, from left to right, Dry-A-Fly Patch, hook-sharpening file, forceps, leader clippers, retractor reel, leader straightener, Extractor snake-bite kit, needlenose pliers, dry-fly floatant and flashlight.

front of your vest with small retractor reels makes them easier to locate and use when needed.

Small locking forceps are very handy when releasing trout by grasping the hook and gently unhooking the trout.

Small needlenose pliers are useful in mashing down barbs on hooks and for other jobs.

Leader straighteners are simple rubber-in-leather holders that are useful for taking the curl out of our leaders and tippets each day before we start fishing, and throughout the day when needed.

Dry-fly floatants which can be applied to dry flies to try to keep them from absorbing water are a must for those who plan to fish dry flies.

In conjunction with the last item, a patch or pad of water-absorbent material is good to have for drying a water-soaked dry fly before dry-fly floatant is applied.

Split shot or heavy wire to apply to the leader to help sink underwater flies are well worth using.

I always carry a Sawyer Extractor snake-bite kit in the back of my vest when I'm fishing in areas where poisonous snakes may live. This has a great suction force, eliminating the need for cutting tissue.

A small waterproof flashlight is nice to have in your vest if you plan to fish late in the evening.

EMERGENCY PACK

In the back of my vest I carry a quart-size zip lock bag with numerous emergency items. These include: a small multi-purpose Swiss army knife, a butane lighter, wader-repair material, rod-repair guides and cement, a referee's whistle, and bandaids.

KNOTS

Fly-fishermen need to be able to depend on their knots, which means one must be able to tie them so that they are consistently strong. The best way to achieve this is to select a small number that will meet your needs, and then practice tying them until you can tie them easily.

Following is a basic selection of knots that will nicely cover many of your needs.

TYING BACKING TO THE REEL

I tie an overhand knot in the end of 20-pound test Dacron backing line and attach this to the reel spool with an Arbor Knot. (This is basically a slip knot which slides down tightly against the reel arbor.) Wind on enough backing to fill about one half of the depth of the spool. Be careful not to add so much backing that the fly line will hit against the reel pillars.

Arbor Knot

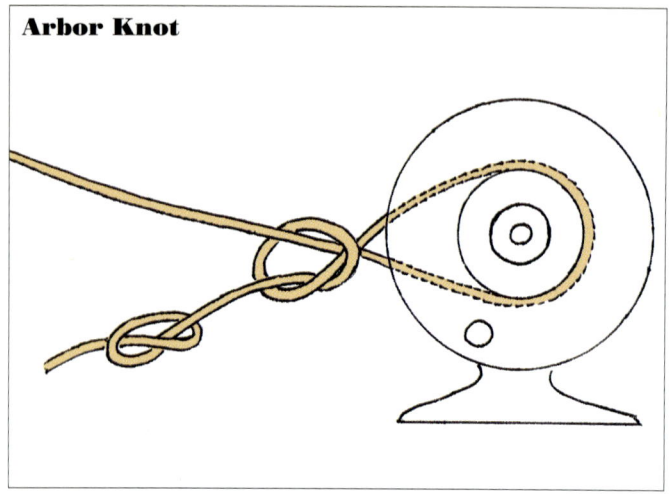

This will damage the finish of the fly line. Reel manufacturers give guidelines as to the amount of backing each reel will hold with different line sizes.

TYING FLY LINE TO BACKING

The Albright Knot is an excellent knot for attaching fly line to backing.

Pull about three feet of the fly line marked "this end to reel" from its plastic spool. Form a loop in the end of the fly line by folding about two inches of the end of the line back over itself. While holding this loop in your left hand, insert about six inches of the backing through this loop, and while holding the backing under your left thumb, begin wrapping the backing toward the end of the loop in the fly line.

Make 10-12 wraps of the backing from left to right with each wrap snug against the previous wrap.

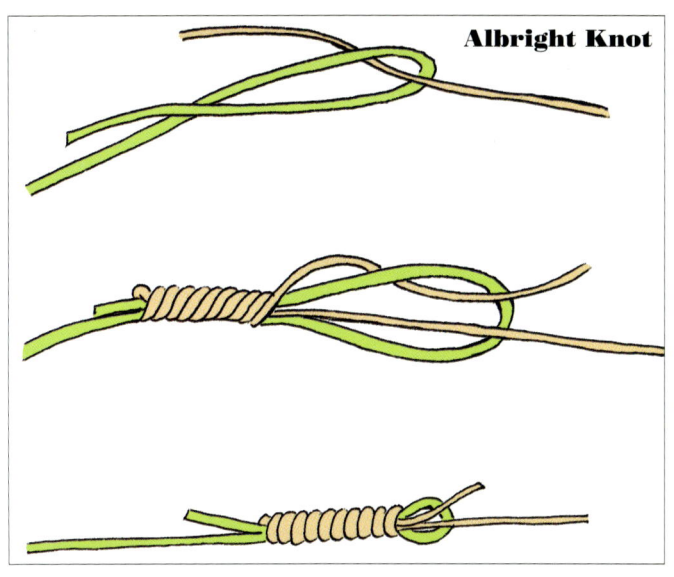

Insert the end of the backing through the loop in the end of the fly line opposite of where it entered originally so that both pieces of the backing come out beside each other.

With your left forefinger and thumb, slide the loops of backing to 1/8 inch from the end of the loop in the fly line. While holding the loops in place with your left forefinger and thumb, pull on the short tag end of the backing to firm up the wraps. Next pull the standing (long) part of the backing, then finally pull both pieces of backing. Trim off the tag end of the fly line and backing.

ATTACHING LEADER TO FLY LINE

After you wind all of the fly line onto the reel, except the last three feet, you are ready to attach the leader to the line.

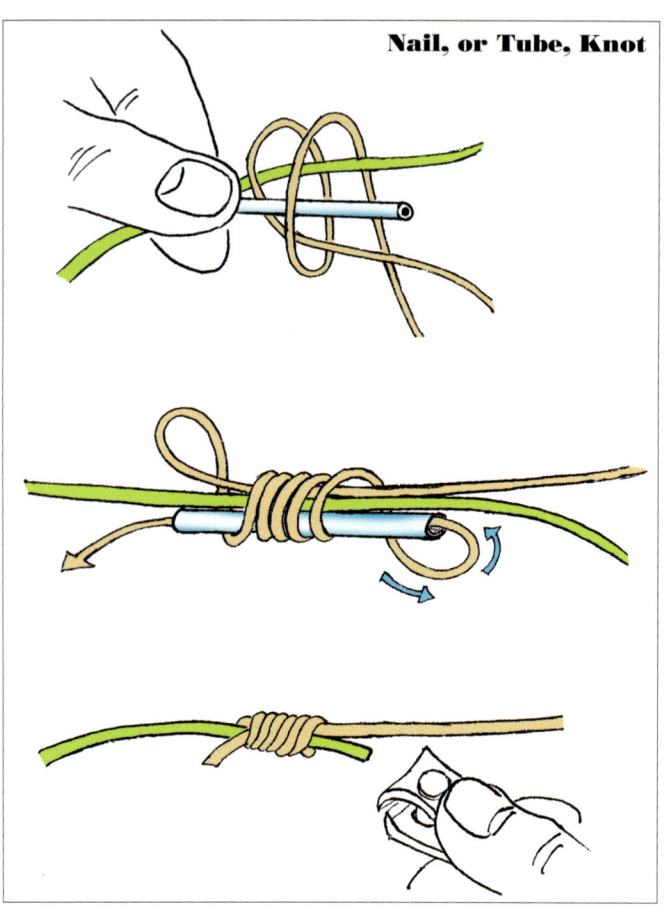

Nail, or Tube, Knot

The nail, or tube, knot is the easiest knot to use to attach your fly line to the leader..

Hold the end of the fly line and the tube between the thumb and forefinger of your left hand with about two inches of the tube and the fly line sticking out to the right. Form a ten-inch loop in the butt of the leader with your right hand. With your left hand hold this loop tight against the tube. Use your right hand to hold the short end of the leader and make five tight wraps to the right over the tube and the fly line so these wraps are tight against each other about 1/2 inch from the end of the fly line.

While holding the wraps in place with your left-hand thumb and forefinger, use your right hand to insert the end of the leader through the tube from right to left. Slide the tube out, and while keeping the wraps in place with your thumbnails, tighten them by pulling the leader on both sides of the knot. Next pull the fly line and leader to lock the knot in place.

Clip off the tag end of the leader and fly line.

Needle Knot

This is an alternate knot for attaching the leader to the fly line. It is similar to the nail knot except the butt of the leader is inserted into the center of the fly line giving a smoother connection.

Shave down about two inches of the butt of the leader with a razor blade to a fine point. Insert a small-diameter needle into the center of the end of the fly line and punch this out of the side of the fly line about 1/4 inch up. Stick the butt of the leader into the eye of the needle and pull this through the fly line so it extends out about six inches.

Place the end of the fly line tight against the needle with the end of the line even with the eye of the needle. Make four tight, snug wraps with the butt of the leader over the line and needle from left to right. Insert the end of the leader into the eye of the needle and pull the needle out to the left being careful to retain the four wraps.

Needle Knot

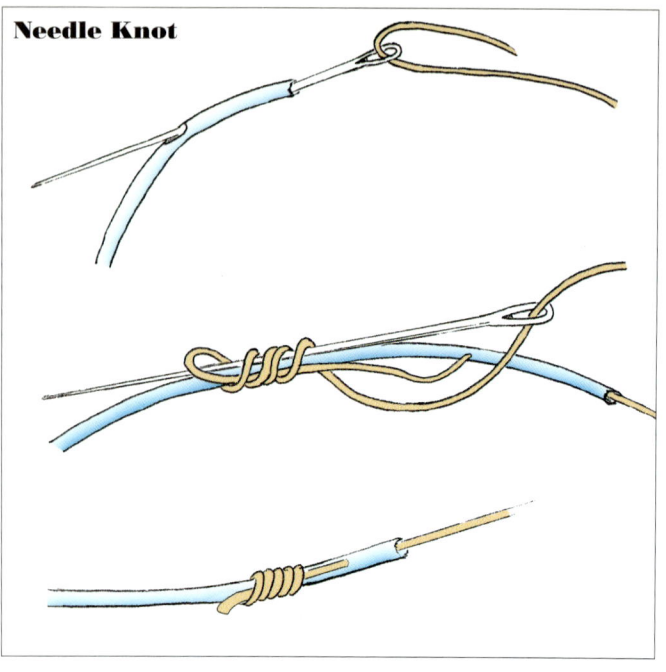

Use your thumbnails to hold the wraps together and slide them toward the point where the fly line sticks out of the side of the fly line. Pull on the leader on both sides of the wraps to lock the knot into place. Trim off the tag end of the leader and the knot is complete. You can coat this with several thin coats of Pliobond or Flexament if you want to make it very smooth.

TYING THE TIPPET TO THE LEADER

The surgeon's knot or a double surgeon's knot—is a strong knot used to attach the tippet to the leader. It's easy to tie, even during low-light levels.

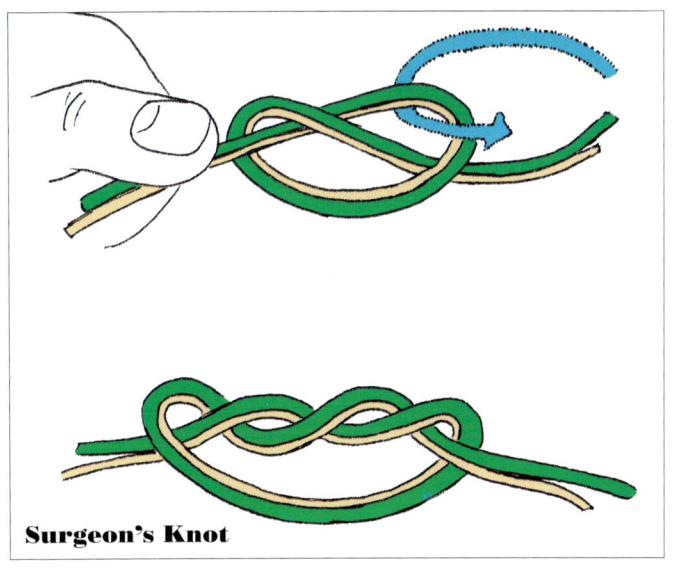

Surgeon's Knot

Clip two to three feet of tippet material from the spool. Allow about five inches of this to lie beside the end of the leader. Form a loop and tie a simple overhand knot, being sure to pull the whole tippet through the loop, along with the end of the leader.

While retaining the open loop with the thumb and forefinger of your left hand, insert the tippet and the end of the leader through the loop the second time.

Pull all four pieces of mono on each side of the knot until it draws down tightly, then clip off the two short ends.

TYING THE FLY TO THE TIPPET

The improved clinch knot is a good knot for tying the fly onto the tippet.

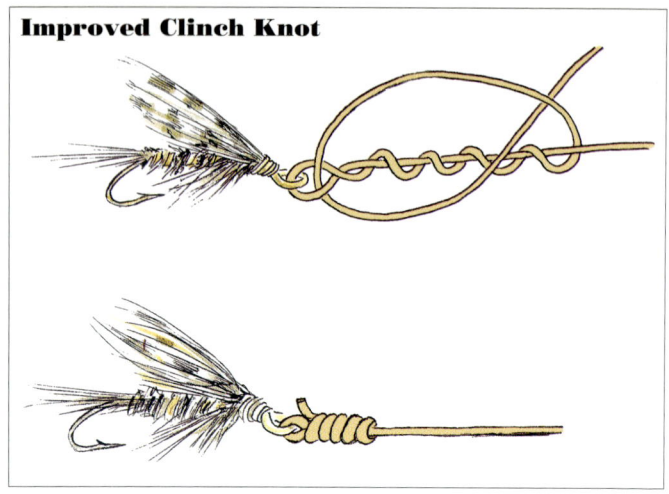

Improved Clinch Knot

Insert about five inches of the tippet through the eye of the fly. Make five wraps of the tag end of the tippet around the standing part of the tippet while holding the fly firmly. Insert the tag end of the tippet through the gap formed immediately in front of the eye of the fly. Pull five inches through this gap, then insert it in the loop over the wraps, and pull gently on the standing part of the tippet.

While holding the fly securely, pull firmly on the standing part of the leader until all of the wraps in the knot draw down tightly.

This is a good selection of knots that will satisfy a broad assortment of fishing situations. By practicing these knots you will become proficient at tying them and can have complete confidence in them.

It is important to test your tippet and fly knots every half hour while you're fishing to make sure they are still holding securely. It's time-consuming if a knot breaks when you test it, but it's much better than having it break while you're fighting the largest trout you've ever hooked.

Most knots break when they slip under pressure and cut themselves. For this reason it is extremely important to pull down each knot very tightly when tying it.

There is a formula which is helpful in determining the tippet size one needs for the various sizes of trout flies. One has some latitude here, but this is a good starting point.

Formula: Fly size divided by 3 (constant) = tippet in X

Example: Size 12 Fly divided by 3 = 4X tippet

Leader Tippet Comparing X Code and Diameter

Leader Tippet (thousandths of an inch)	X Code	Pound Test (approximate)
.003	8X	1
.004	7X	2
.005	6X	3
.006	5X	4
.007	4X	6
.008	3X	8
.009	2X	10
.010	1X	12
.011	0X	14

Leader Formulas
(for building your own leaders)
Murray's Classic Leader Formulas™ 9 feet

9 ft., 2X leader	9 ft., 3X leader	9ft., 4X leader	9ft., 5X leader	9ft., 6X leader
.022/36	.022/30	.022/30	.022/30	.022/30
.020/18	.020/18	.020/18	.020/12	.020/12
.017/12	.017/12	.017/12	.017/12	.017/12
.015/6	.015/6	.015/6	.015/6	.015/6
.013/6	.013/6	.013/6	.013/6	.013/6
.011/6	.011/6	.011/6	.011/6	.011/6
.009/24	.009/6	.009/6	.009/6	.009/6
	.008/24	.007/24	.007/6	.007/6
			.006/24	.005/24

FLY TACKLE

Murray's Classic Leader Formulas 7 ½ ft.

7 ½ ft., 2X leader	7 ½ ft., 3X leader	7 ½ ft., 4X leader	7 ½ ft., 5X leader
.022/24	.022/24	.022/24	.022/24
.020/18	.020/12	.020/12	.020/12
.017/6	.017/6	.017/6	.017/6
.015/6	.015/6	.015/6	.015/6
.013/6	.013/6	.013/6	.013/6
.011/6	.011/6	.011/6	.011/6
.009/24	.009/6	.009/6	.009/6
	.008/24	.007/24	.007/6
			.006/18

Murray's Bright Butt Leader Formulas

9 ft., 2X leader	9 ft., 3X leader	9ft., 4X leader	9ft., 5X leader	9ft., 6X leader
Red 25# Amnesia 36	Red 25# Amnesia 36	Red 25# Amnesia 36	Red 25# Amnesia 36	Red 25# Amnesia 36
Red 20# Amnesia 24	Red 20# Amnesia 24	Red 20# Amnesia 24	Red 20# Amnesia 18	Red 20# Amnesia 18
Umpqua .015 12	Umpqua .015 6	Umpqua .015 6	Umpqua .015 6	Umpqua .015 6
Umpqua .013 6	Umpqua .013 6	Umpqua .013 6	Umpqua .013 6	Umpqua .013 6
Umpqua .011 6	Umpqua .011 6	Umpqua .011 6	Umpqua .011 6	Umpqua .011 6
Umpqua .009 24	Umpqua .009 6	Umpqua .009 6	Umpqua .009 6	Umpqua .009 6
	Umpqua .008 24	Umpqua .007 24	Umpqua .007 6	Umpqua .007 6
			Umpqua .006 24	Umpqua .005 24

Murray's Bright Butt Leader (9ft. 4X with one indicator)

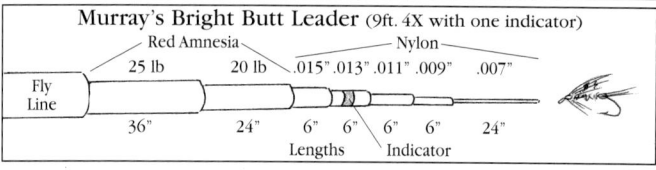

Chapter 3

FLY CASTING

Learning to cast a trout fly delicately and accurately is an essential part of fly-fishing for trout. Fortunately, I've learned through the schools that I conduct each year that one can easily achieve this.

The majority of beginning students in my schools have never cast with a fly rod before, but they catch on very quickly. After about 15 minutes of instruction and practice they understand the basics and are well on their way to being able to enjoy the pleasure of fly-fishing.

Let's begin on the lawn and you'll see how easy fly casting is.

Pull about 30 feet of fly line from the reel, out through the guides, and lay this out on the lawn in front of you.

With the rod tip pointed straight down the line, slightly lower the tip towards the ground. Grasp the line firmly in your line hand.

With the wrist of your rod-hand locked, smoothly bring the fly rod up to about ten o'clock by lifting your forearm.

At this point, snap your wrist back firmly so the rod accelerates back to 12 o'clock, sending the fly line high into the air behind you. It is very important that one use enough power on the back cast to fully extend the line behind you. The best way to assure that you are doing this properly is to actually turn and watch your line to be sure it's high and straight behind you.

With the fly line extended behind you, begin your forward cast by snapping your wrist forward and starting to move your forearm forward.

As the fly line accelerates forward, continue pushing firmly with your forearm, and finally follow through by turning the tip of the fly rod over so the cast will be delivered straight and delicately.

If you find you need to make longer casts, shoot the line forward by applying extra power as you push the rod forward and release the slack line from your line hand as the line accelerates forward. However, be careful about fishing too long a line because the extra line on the water can produce "drag" on the fly causing it to act unnaturally and the trout may refuse to take it. On the type of streams we're discussing, experienced anglers catch more trout with casts under 40 feet than they do with casts over 40 feet.

THE ROLL CAST

When one is fishing in a location where there are trees or a steep bank behind you that prevents a conventional back cast, the roll cast will enable you to easily cast your fly out in front of you.

With the fly line on the water in front of you, while holding the line firmly in your line hand, lift the fly rod to the 10 o'clock position over your shoulder. Stop here and allow the fly line on the water to come to a complete stop. Raise the fly rod by fully extending your rod arm and move it forward to the 1 o'clock position. Begin your forward cast here by pushing the rod tip forcefully forward to the 2 o'clock position. The fly line will be pulled from the water and will roll forward in front of you. After the loop of the fly line begins turning over in front of you, drop the rod tip to 3 o'clock and the fly will be neatly delivered in front of you.

On very small trout streams—where I often find trout feeding on the surface just 15 feet upstream of where I'm standing—I use a much simplified version of the roll cast. This consists of holding the fly in my line hand with the line hanging from the rod tip down to the fly. I move in cautiously holding the rod tip at about 11 o'clock in front of me. When I'm at a location from which I believe I can get a natural drift with my fly, I snap the rod tip forward and release the fly a split second later. With a little practice you'll become very accurate with this presentation and the lack of the need for false casting will enable you to catch many wary trout that you could not take otherwise.

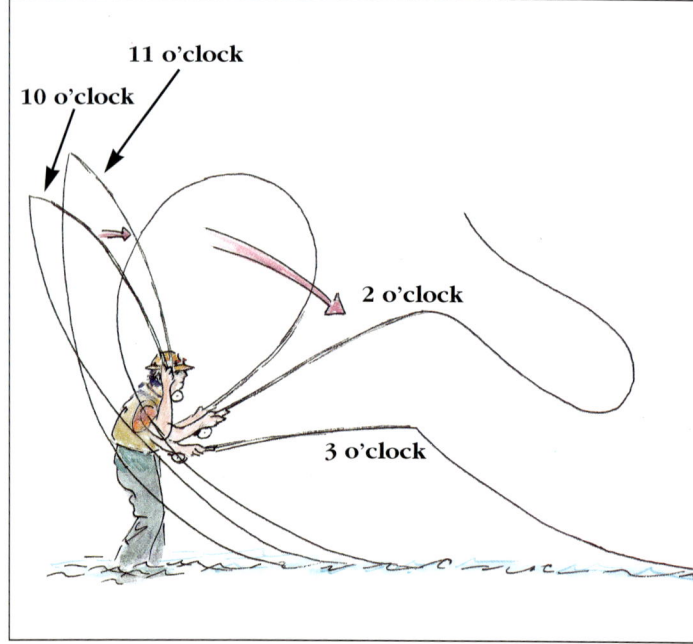

Chapter 4

NATURAL TROUT FOODS

Trout feed on a broad variety of natural foods. In fact, on many small trout streams there are few heavy hatches of specific aquatic insects and thus the trout are opportunistic. They will feed on any natural insects that drift down the stream.

There are, however, occasions when the trout are selective in what they want to feed on and this challenge requires we give some careful consideration to the fly we plan to use. Now, before you get scared—assuming you'll need four years of college entomology and two years of Latin before you can intelligently choose the correct fly to "match the hatch"—I'll show you an option.

Mayflies are an important food source for trout on many streams. Thick hatches excite both trout and anglers.

Mayfly Hatches (East)

Insect	Hatching Period					Matching Fly
	March	April	May	June	July	
Epeorus pleuralis	■	■				Quill Gordon 12, 14 Mr. Rapidan 12, 14
Paraleptophlebia adaptiva		■	■			Blue Quill 16, 18
Stenonema vicarium		■	■			March Brown 12, 14 Mr. Rapidan 12, 14
Stenonema fuscum			■			Grey Fox 14 Ginger Quill 14
Stenonema canadense			■	■		Light Cahill 14 Grey Yellow No Hackle 16
Ephemerella dorothea				■		Fox Sulphur 16, 18 Grey Yellow No Hackle 16, 18

Mayfly Hatches (Midwest)

Insect	Hatching Period							Matching Fly
	April	May	June	July	Aug.	Sept.	Oct.	
Ephemerella subvaria		■						Hendrickson 14
Ephemerella dorothea			■	■				Sulphur 16
Ephemera simulans			■					Brown Drake 14
Pseudocloeon				■		■		Tiny Olive 20, 24
Tricorythodes				■	■			Trico Spinner 22, 24
Beatis		■	■	■	■	■		Blue Wing Olive 18, 20

Mayfly Hatches (West)

Insect	Hatching Period							Matching Fly
	April	May	June	July	Aug.	Sept.	Oct.	
Epeorus (various)			■	■				Slate Drake 14
Ephemerella (various)			■	■	■			Pale Morning Dun 18
Heptagenia				■	■	■	■	Western Gray Drake 14
Ephemerella grandis			■					Western Green Drake 10
Callibaetis		■			■			Specked Spinner 16
Tricorythodes				■	■			Trico Spinner 20, 22
Beatis		■	■	■	■	■		Blue Wing Olive 18, 20

My old trout tutor was one of the most accomplished anglers I've ever known. Jack could catch trout under the most demanding conditions, even when other fishermen failed. His basic belief was that, "If you want to catch trout consistently, try to duplicate what nature is doing." I really don't think Jack could distinguish a mayfly from a caddisfly but when he saw insects on the water which he suspected the trout were feeding on he would match these in color and size with his flies. That is, if he saw small yellow flies on the water he'd choose a small yellow artificial fly from his fly box and fish with it. This is a very sound approach and is very effective.

Personally, I enjoy going into a little more depth so we'll look at some of the basic aquatic insect hatches throughout the country.

STONEFLIES

Stoneflies are another group of insects that trout feed upon. These insects can range from the small dark stoneflies one often

Adult stoneflies are a mouthful for trout, but most often trout feed on nymphs.

sees on snowbanks along the streams early in the season, to the giant stoneflies reaching an inch-and-a-half long.

Trout get their best chance to feed upon these insects when nymphs move out into the shallows and when the adult females return to lay eggs. The one exception to this is the little yellow stonefly which hatches on some of the headwater mountain trout streams in varying concentrations from late spring until late in the summer. Possibly because of the longevity of the hatch, trout always seem to be willing to take a size 16 Little Yellow Stonefly dry fly when these flies are hatching.

I have not found it necessary to duplicate the stoneflies with my fly patterns on hatches other than the little yellow stonefly hatch.

CADDISFLIES

There are a broad variety of caddisflies on the different types of trout streams that we're discussing. The predominate colors of the adults are olive and brown.

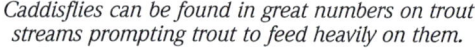

Caddisflies can be found in great numbers on trout streams prompting trout to feed heavily on them.

One of the finest anglers I've ever known fishes a Dry Elk Hair Caddis with an olive or brown body from size 18 to 14 for all of these hatches. He insists that usually he gets good results with these two patterns.

Many anglers have also found that a basic selection of underwater patterns will meet their needs for caddis larva and pupa fishing. Popular flies here include the Hare's Ear Nymph, Red Squirrel Nymph, Olive Caddis Pupa and Bright Green Caddis Pupa all in sizes 12 to 18.

TERRESTRIAL INSECTS

Land-born insects play a very important role in the diet of trout, especially in small streams. The lack of large numbers of aquatic

Terrestrial insects are an important source of food for trout, especially during summer when hatches of aquatic insects are sparse.

insects on these streams, and the ever-present overhead tree canopy that seems to rain terrestrial insects on the stream, are the two major factors accounting for this. I've seen some headwater streams in which the trout appeared to live almost completely on terrestrials because the streams were not rich enough to produce many aquatic insects.

As you would expect, these trout will feed on almost any terrestrial which comes their way, but there is a natural sequence in which these insects appear around the stream which will give you a general guide as to which patterns to fish when.

Black ants show up surprisingly early on many of these streams (during April in the Southeast), followed by cinnamon ants, then beetles, next crickets and finally grasshoppers. From midsummer until when freezing conditions hit in the fall, these will all be around the streams at the same time and trout can feed on them all. There are a few tactical tricks, though, which can be helpful that we'll investigate in the chapter on summer fishing.

My favorite terrestrial fly patterns include Black Fur Ants sizes 14 to 18, Cinnamon Fur Ants sizes 14 to18, Mr. Rapidan Ant sizes 14 to 18, Crowe Beetle sizes 12 to 18, Murray's Flying Beetle sizes 14 to 16, Shenk's Cricket sizes 12 to 16, Shenk's Hopper sizes 12 to 16, and Dave's Hopper sizes 10 to 14.

MINNOWS

Minnows become an important part of a trout's diet especially in the larger streams we're discussing. Since trout feeding on minnows seem to take whatever they can get to first, it is seldom necessary to play a match-the-minnow game with streamer selection.

Sculpins and other minnows provide trout with many easy meals.

Depending upon the stream, trout feed on sculpins, dace, chubs, shiners and a variety of other minnows as well. My basic streamer selection (for use all across the country) includes: Whitlock's Sculpin, Murray's Sculpin, Shenk's White Streamer, White Marabou Muddlers, Strymphs in both olive and black and Woolly Buggers in both olive and black. This selection—in sizes 6, 8, and 10—covers all of my needs.

BASIC FLY SELECTIONS

The following three fly plates show basic fly selections that will cover the majority of your fly-angling needs across the country.

Eastern Fly Selection

Royal Wulff
size 16

March Brown
size 14

Adams Parachute
size 16

Mr. Rapidan
Parachute
size 14

Elk Hair
Caddis
size 16

Shenk's Cricket
size 14

Murray's Flying
Beetle
size 16

Hare's Ear
Nymph
size 12

Squirrel Nymph
size 14

Black Woolly
Bugger - size 10

Murray's Olive
Strymph - size 10

Skenk's Sculpin
size 8

Midwest Fly Selection

Royal Wulff
size 14

Light Humpy
size 14

Adams Parachute
size 16

Elk Hair Caddis
size 16

Black Fur Ant
size 16

Dave's Hopper
size 12

Prince Nymph
size 14

Hare's Ear
Nymph - size 12

Brooks' Dark
Stonefly Nymph
size 8

Black Woolly
Bugger
size 8

Murray's Olive
Strymph
size 10

Whitlock's Sculpin
size 6

NATURAL TROUT FOODS

Western Fly Selection

Royal Wulff
size 14

Light Humpy
size 16

Adams Parachute
size 16

Olive Stimulator
size 14

Dave's Hopper
size 12

Shenk's Cricket
size 14

Black Fur Ant
size 16

Hare's Ear Nymph
size 12

Prince Nymph
size 14

Red Squirrel Nymph
size 14

Black Woolly Bugger
size 10

Whitlock's Sculpin
size 6

Chapter 5

READING THE WATER

Learning to read the water in order to accurately identify potential feeding stations trout may select in the stream is the single most valuable skill an angler can develop. Once you have this information, you will know where to drift your flies so trout will see them and, hopefully, take them.

Fortunately, this is a skill one can learn fairly easily because most of these trout streams do not have an overabundance of food for the fish. Consequently, trout must feed whenever there is food available and they must do it in an efficient manner. This means they will select feeding stations that are fairly close to main currents in the pools because this is where insects will

Six feeding stations in a mountain trout-stream pool.

READING THE WATER • 43

drift. However, the trout need something to block the full force of the current so they can easily hold their positions.

In order to help you learn how to read the water, let's look at the six potential feeding stations which one may find in typical mountain trout streams. Few pools will have all six of these feeding stations, but many pools will have several of them.

Since we fish these small headwater streams by wading upstream in order to prevent scaring the trout, let's set up a pool which has all six feeding stations and fish it from its downstream end to its head.

The lip is the first feeding station we come to as we approach a pool from downstream. This is formed when one or more boulders or large stones momentarily dam or slow the main current before it drops down to the pool below.

Trout usually hold immediately in front of this boulder and sip in any natural insects which drift by. I think of this as the "primary" feeding station in the pool, meaning it usually holds the largest trout in the pool.

The lip is an easy feeding station to fish. If you use a low, cautious approach and stay well below it, you can cast a dry fly several feet above it. And by holding the rod tip high, get a natural drift, and catch the trout. With a little practice, you'll be able to accurately discern, within less than a foot, where this trout will hold.

The tail of the pool is the feeding station which is located just upstream of the lip. It is not as easy to pinpoint where the trout will hold here because often the only protection they can find are depressions in the stream bottom. The tail feeding station is at its best if there is no well-defined lip.

I fish this area by staying well below the lip of the pool so I don't scare the trout. I use about four casts, spaced about three feet apart from left to right, and cover the entire area. It is not necessary to drift your fly over any one spot more than once, because if a trout sees it and doesn't take it on the first drift, it means either you have spooked it or you had too much drag, making the fly act unnaturally. In either case, you could show it to him a dozen more times and he will not take it.

The mid-pool feeding station is located in the middle of the pool beginning just upstream of the tail. In most small streams few large trout locate here to feed because the main features blocking the current are located on the bottom of the stream. This means a trout holding here will have to swim through the entire water column, often three feet or more, to feed on an insect drifting on the surface.

The one exception is when a major flood in the past has shoved a large boulder into the middle of the pool. If the current

Learning to "read the water" to identify various feeding stations is the most valuable skill a trout angler can master.

comes directly at this boulder, slows momentarily, then slides around it, you have a good feeding station for the trout. A nice trout can hold in the protected area in front of this boulder and easily pick off any natural insects drifting by.

I fish the mid-pool area by drifting my fly across the main currents—which may take from three to ten drifts—depending upon the size of the pool.

After I've fished the mid-pool area, I carefully examine the sides of the pool to see if there is a back eddy present which may hold feeding trout. The back eddy is usually located tight against the bank and is manifested to us by a reverse current against the bank. (Yes, the current is actually flowing upstream.) These back eddies can range from card-table size to automobile size but they all have one thing in common: the trout are always in the reverse flow, looking downstream to intercept any insects that are riding on the stream.

The most dependable way I've found to fish a back eddy is to actually spot the trout then go one-on-one with him. Seeing a trout in a back eddy often is not difficult. If you can spot a rise form-where a trout actually sucks an insect from the surface-you move in slowly, staying low, and in many cases you can see the trout. Once you've spotted him you cast your fly about two feet up-current from him and allow the current to deliver the fly.

The head of the pool is the feeding station which holds the most food. Many mayfly and stonefly nymphs and caddis larva live in this well-aerated water. In order to feed efficiently, most of the trout move to the sides of the heavy current and locate themselves right where the fast water meets the slow water. These flows are usually fairly uniform as they roll into the main part of the pool making them easy to fish effectively. Come in directly below these runs and cast a dry fly straight upstream along the interface of the currents. By fishing the lower area first, then gradually lengthening your casts, you can usually catch several trout here.

The corner is the last feeding station I fish in the pool. If the largest trout in the pool was not on the lip he is here because he can get a tremendous amount to eat with very little effort on his part.

The corner is a miniature lazy Susan that forms on one side of the head of the pool where the fast riffle pushes down into the main part of the pool. Because of the bottom composition in the downstream portion of the pool, all of the water cannot flow smoothly on downstream. A portion of this water is turned to the side of the pool and is almost siphoned back upstream along the bank. It hits a large boulder here where it shunts across its face to return back out into the main part of the stream. The trout lies in this corner feeding station right beside

When streams are a little high, large trout are often caught in the corners of a pool.

the boulder and facing in toward the bank sips in every insect that drifts by.

The corner is an easy feeding station to fish if you use caution and approach it from the center of the stream. I use a cast of about ten feet and instantly get my rod tip high in the air in order to bridge the fast currents. A natural drift of about a foot is usually enough to catch this trout.

This understanding of where the trout will hold and feed in small streams carries over quite well to larger streams when one plans to fish dry flies and small nymphs.

MEDIUM-SIZE STREAMS

In medium-size streams—those reaching 100 feet wide—the riffles entering the pools are much wider and have more force than the headwater streams just mentioned and the mid-pool areas are much longer, wider and deeper. To give you an idea of the streams which I'm referring to as medium-size so that you can apply this information to streams in your area, here are a few that come to mind: the West Branch of the Saranac River in New York, Penns Creek in Pennsylvania, Big Stoney Creek in Virginia's Shenandoah Valley, the Oconaluftee River in the Smokies, the Bechler in the southwest corner of the Yellowstone National Park, and the West Gallatin in the lower canyon in Montana.

These streams are large enough to allow anglers to wade downstream without scaring the trout, so let's examine these feeding stations by starting at the head of the pool and working our way downstream.

The shallow riffle close to the bank holds a good population of small aquatic nymphs and larvae. Many small trout feed here all day and larger trout move in to feed in the low-light levels early in the morning and late in the evening.

One approaches this area from below and fishes it the same way one would the small headwater streams with dry flies and nymphs. (A)

The deep riffle in the middle of the stream is attractive to large rainbow trout. These areas frequently hold good popula-

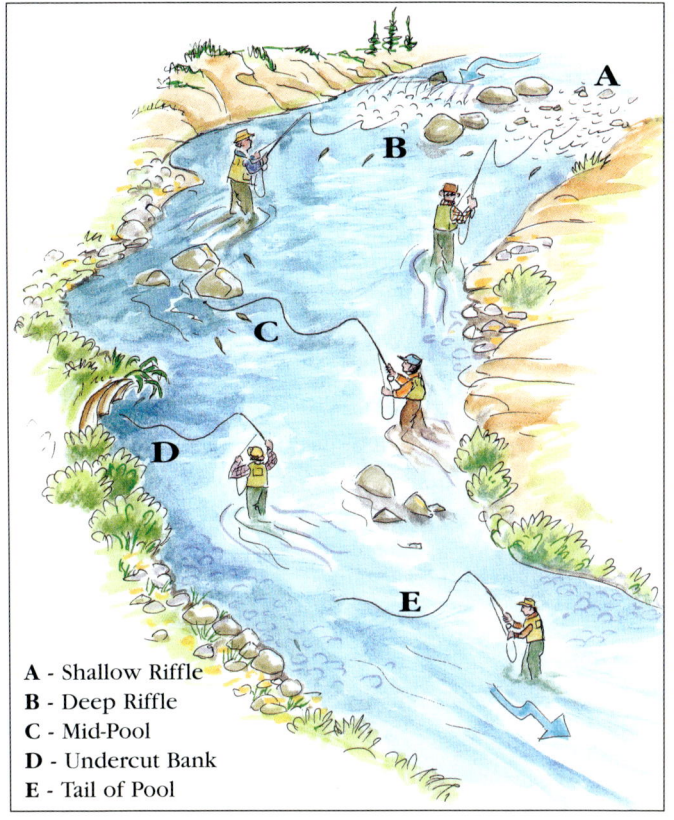

A - Shallow Riffle
B - Deep Riffle
C - Mid-Pool
D - Undercut Bank
E - Tail of Pool

tions of large stonefly nymphs and can be fished effectively with the swinging nymphing method we'll cover later. (B)

The mid-pool area often contains good populations of minnows and this is a good place to fish streamers which match them. Wading down the side of the pool, I cast a streamer straight across the stream and after giving it time to sink I use a very slow hand-stripping action to swim the fly across the stream bottom. By wading slowly downstream and continuing to fish my streamers in this manner, I can usually catch several nice trout from each of these areas. (C)

Some medium-size streams have undercut banks that provide both feeding stations and resting areas for the trout. Frequently these will be located at the outside of the elbow in a curve of the stream. However, sometimes they are located in a straight portion of the pool where an almost imperceptible swinging current has cut back under the bank.

The West Gallatin River in Yellowstone National Park is a typical medium-size stream in its lower reaches. Streamer fishing is often very productive in these streams.

Undercut banks can be fished effectively with nymphs or drys from below or across stream, and with streamers from across stream as well. I devote extra time to undercut banks because the food, cover and shade that they provide often attract some of the largest trout. Frequently, they are especially appealing to any large brown trout in the area. (D)

The tail of the pool in these medium-size streams often hold large trout late in the evening that move in to feed on minnows. The same streamer tactics which are effective in the mid-pool area work quite well here. Additionally, I've had excellent fishing

Experiment with dry flies, nymphs, and streamers on medium-size streams because one may be more productive than the other depending upon existing conditions.

for cutthroats that often locate on the sides of the tails of pools to feed on adult aquatic insects when there are good hatches. (E)

HIGH-MEADOW STREAMS

The feeding stations trout select in meandering high-meadow streams overlap with those they select in the two types of streams just mentioned, and I fish them accordingly.

Reading the water to determine likely feeding stations can help the angler to catch many large trout.

For example, the edges of the riffle entering the pool can give great dry-fly fishing just like those same areas in a headwater mountain stream. (A)

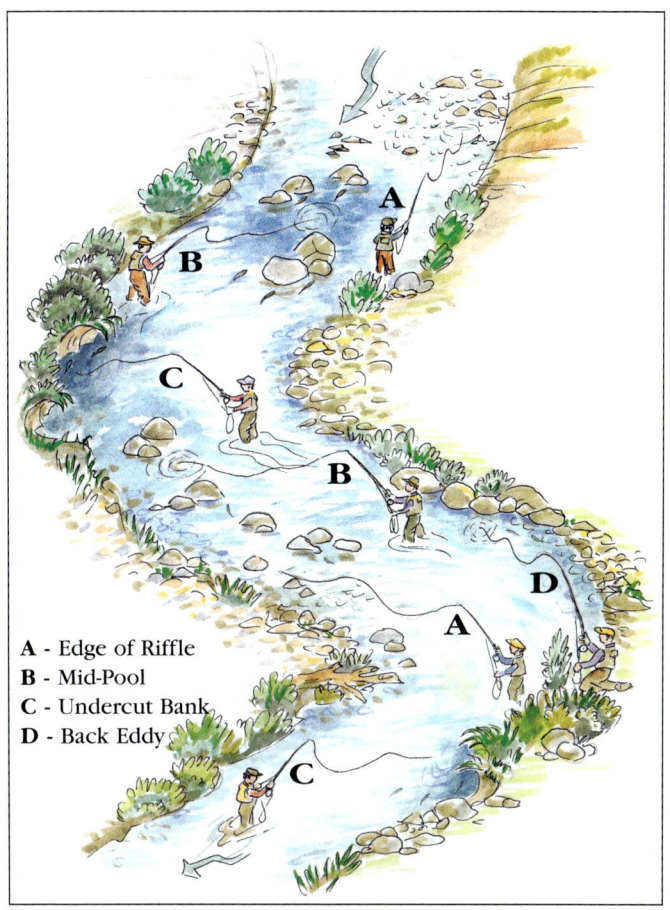

A - Edge of Riffle
B - Mid-Pool
C - Undercut Bank
D - Back Eddy

If there are deep cuts in the mid-pool area you can catch these trout by fishing across stream to them with streamers just like we did in the larger streams. The main difference is that on a high meadow stream we may have to use a hands and knees approach to prevent scaring the trout. (B)

Undercut banks in meadow streams often hold some of the largest trout. On numerous occasions, these areas are the feeding stations that produce the largest cutthroats on each of these streams in Yellowstone National Park. If I spot a trout feeding on the surface along one of these undercut banks, I try to match the natural aquatic insects with a dry fly and drift this over him. If I do not see a feeding trout, I like to drift a dry grasshopper pattern over the undercut. (C)

Frequently, small back eddies are valuable feeding stations in meadow streams. The trout here are usually very wary but I usually take some of my best trout in these areas by crawling up the banks and placing a gentle cast dead center on the first cast. This normally results in a good strike or else a spooked trout. Only on long back eddies, tight to undercut banks, do I expect to catch more than one trout. (D)

After you've fished several hundred yards of your first meadow stream you'll realize these meandering gems are a repeating series of gentle riffles, mid-pool cuts, undercut banks and back eddies with just enough variation thrown in to keep you on your toes and to make the fish very exciting to stalk.

Reading the water to correctly identify the specific locations where trout will choose to feed definitely will give you a great advantage when you try to catch them. However, regardless of how proficient you become at discerning the feeding stations, the trout frequently seem to make subtle adaptations which require that you stay observant and adapt your tactics if you are to outsmart them.

Chapter 6

SPOTTING TROUT

One of my favorite trout-fishing tactics is to spot a trout in the stream and then move in very cautiously to drift a dry fly over it, catching it if possible.

There are several physical aids that are very helpful in this endeavor. A hat or cap with a dark under-brim that cuts down the glare and shades your eyes is the first good investment. Subdued colored clothing that enables you to approach trout so that you can get close enough to see them without their getting scared is a wise choice. Another important suggestion that will

Learning to spot trout and going one on one with them is a very exciting and gratifying tactic.

allow you to see trout is a pair of polarized sunglasses. These let you see clearly through the glare on the surface of the stream, allowing you to spot trout.

Your greatest ally, though, in being able to see trout in the stream is always the knowledge that it is possible. Making a conscientious effort to see them is the second part of the equation.

Before I get into the mechanics of how to achieve this, I need to point out that I am not talking about seeing the trout which you scare and see running for cover as you walk up to the stream. True, you can clearly see many of these trout holding close to the stream bottom in the deepest part of the pool, but few if any of these trout are catchable and fishing for them is usually a waste of time.

In order to see the trout in their feeding stations, I move in as close as possible to a pool, trying hard not to move quickly because I believe it is possible to do this without scaring the fish. I pause for a few minutes and slowly scan the whole pool very carefully. Very seldom do I see a trout lying before me as we see in photographs or paintings. Rather, what I'm looking for is some visual trigger that will signal the presence of a trout and thus prompt me to investigate that specific area more closely.

The first trigger to look out for which will alerts you to the presence of a trout is their movement. This can be either a subtle movement as he turns to feed on a natural nymph drifting in the current, or else the fish slightly changing their feeding position.

Frequently, I'm not too sure whether I have actually seen something that indicates the presence of a trout or whether it is just my imagination driven by my wishful thinking. However, once I see something which I suspect might be a trout I examine it very carefully for as long as it takes to determine if it's a

Skilled anglers use a low, cautious approach to move in closely so they can spot the trout without scaring them.

trout or not. If it is a trout, I go ahead and fish for it by casting my fly two feet upstream from the fish. If it is not a trout, I either look for one in other places in the pool, or else I go ahead and fish the good-looking feeding stations we discussed in the last chapter.

The color of trout can be another visual trigger that I use to help me see where they are in the stream.

Brightly-colored rainbow trout lying over brown cobblestone stream bottoms are easy to see when they are well beyond the distance that you could scare them from, thus giving you a good chance to catch them.

Brook trout are especially easy to see in this way. The bright ivory edges on their fins are one of the most beautiful features in all of nature and they certainly enhance the striking appearance of this fine trout. However, they are also a giveaway to their locations.

I can still see in my mind's eye one of the largest brook trout I've every caught. The sun illuminated his brilliant ivory fins as he held over a dark stony bottom high in Virginia's Blue Ridge Mountains.

The shading contrast of the trout is another visual trigger which has often helped me see trout in the stream. A dark cutthroat trout holding over a bottom composed of light pea-size gravel beside an undercut bank is easy to see. Likewise, one of the largest rainbows I've ever caught I spotted on the Madison River because his light color seemed out of place over the dark rocky bottom behind a car-size boulder.

The contrast in shape requires a little more keen observation on our part but it's another visual trigger which can help you locate trout. The square edge of a brook trout's tail against a round stone bottom, or the elongated shape of a big brown trout over a sandy bottom should prompt us to investigate our suspicions further. Or even better, the tapered head

Charley Waterman enjoys outstanding fishing in beaver ponds by watching closely to spot trout before making his presentations.

of a huge brown trout I spotted sticking out from the straight edge of an old lava flow on the Firehole River quickly let me locate him.

On sunny days, the shadow the trout casts on the stream bottom is often an easier visual trigger to spot than the trout itself. In some cases, the coloration of a trout may blend so well with that of the stream bottom that he may be almost impossible to spot, but there is no hiding his shadow.

Sometimes there are little tricks you can use which will help you see the trout's shadow.

For example, one beautiful fall day Charley Waterman and I were fishing up a small stream in Montana's Crazy

Mountains when we came to a small beaver dam. Charley was very familiar with the stream and knew there were some large trout in this beaver dam so we tried to spot them. Finally, Charley exclaimed as he pointed with his fly rod, "There's a good one tight to the bank just below those willows." Following Charley's point as best I could, I just couldn't see the trout. Even his encouragement to look for the trout's shadow didn't help. Finally Charley suggested, "Squint your eyes. It helps eliminate confusing colors." He was correct. Right away I spotted the trout's shadow and was able to take him on a dry fly.

But there was also the morning when a trout's shadow made a monkey out of me. It was late in the summer and my favorite little mountain brook trout stream was very low and clear. It was about nine o'clock in the morning and the fishing had been very good when I saw my trout and I went one-on-one with it.

As I approached a long narrow pool I could not see any trout in the lower reaches of the pool, but finally I spotted a dandy way up at the head of the pool. He was even feeding. He took several nymphs on each side of him and he always returned to the same spot. Finally, I cast a dry fly upstream and my fly drifted right over him, nothing. Two more good drifts failed to bring even a look. I was totally at a loss until he rose and took a natural insect from the surface four feet to the side of where I'd been drifting my fly. Finally, I realized I'd been fishing to his shadow which the low sun had focused four feet to the side of the trout. He had not even seen my fly. I readjusted my aim and he took my fly on the first drift.

Seeing the trout in the stream is certainly an excellent way to improve your fishing. And personally, I find it to be one of the most exciting forms of trout fishing.

Chapter 7

EARLY-SEASON TACTICS

HEADWATER STREAMS

After long winters of little or no trout fishing, many anglers become impatient and head to trout streams before conditions are ideal. If you find yourself in this category the headwater streams are where to start.

Admittedly, you can't control the high water levels or the cold stream temperatures you often find early in the season, but there are some ways you can work around these environmental stream characteristics on smaller mountain streams.

For example, suppose you drive into the lower reaches of your favorite stream and find the water level is much higher

Headwater trout streams can provide good fishing quite early in the season for the angler willing to drift his nymph along the stream bottom.

than you had hoped it would be. How can you find a fishable water level? Naturally, this depends on the specific stream, but here are two methods I've used with great success.

Many of these streams have numerous small hollows that enter them all along their lengths and early in the season each of these contributes a small amount of water to the stream. By simply hiking several miles up the mountain on trails that parallel most of these streams you can usually find a much lower water level, enabling you to encounter better fishing.

Here is a similar ploy which I often use to find a good stream level if the lower reaches are too high. If you know your stream from past experience, or have a topo map, you may know where a substantial feeder stream enters the main stream upstream. By hiking up to where it enters your stream, you can either fish above it, or fish the feeder itself. This latter option has given me outstanding fishing on many occasions.

Good maps and a compass are helpful if you plan to hike cross-country to remote streams.

62 • TROUT STREAM FLY-FISHING

Another way to beat the high-water game if your specific stream has a mountain road that crosses or comes close to the upper reaches of your stream is to drive up here, park, and hike in to the head of the stream. If you are hiking cross-country—where there is no trail to reach the stream—it is wise to carry a topo map and compass, or at the very least be very observant of the surroundings so that you can find your way back to your car.

Low water temperatures early in the season can hold back the metabolic needs of trout and they may not feed very actively. Brook trout usually do well when the water temperature reaches 40 degrees, but other trout become active at about 45 degrees. A trick I use on the streams I regularly fish is to take the water temperature of each small feeder spring and brook that enters my stream whenever I'm on them, even during the summer. Many of these come from well below ground and may contribute water that is 50 degrees, which is quite significant, if the main stream is 37 degrees.

Even if you are fishing a stream for the first time you can check the temperatures of these feeders in order to locate the best fishing. I've even done this on feeders that cross trails along the streams where I'm hiking.

Topo maps usually show these springs along the streams and can tip you off to those stretches where you can find warmer water. The way I take advantage of this is to fish that portion of the main stream below where the warm feeders enter.

EARLY-SEASON NYMPHING ON SMALL STREAMS

Many anglers use nymphs a great deal early in the season. Their justification for showing trout an imitation of underwater forms of aquatic insects is that even if trout don't want to feed aggressively, they may not be able to resist a nymph drifted right by their noses.

Upstream Dead-Drift Nymph Fishing

This is an excellent technique to use when the stream is so small or so shallow that wading downstream would scare the trout.

Step 1: The nymph is cast upstream to a spot about five feet above where you expect the trout to be.

Step 2: The slack line is stripped in with the line hand as the nymph drifts downstream.

Step 3: Watch the indicator closely for the trout's take, then set the hook quickly.

There are two problems we confront as we prepare to fish dead-drifted nymphs upstream. The first one involves getting the nymphs deep down where trout are holding. Naturally, we use weighted nymphs or add weight to leaders. However, by casting straight upstream, or up and across stream at only a very slight angle, it is easy to drift a nymph along the stream bottom.

The second problem you confront when fishing nymphs is detecting strikes. In most cases, you are compelled to wade and fish upstream in these small streams to prevent scaring the trout. This means you should rely on seeing strikes on your indicator system quickly before the trout detects it as a phony and ejects it. You'll have about a second to a second-and-a-half to set the hook.

My favorite indicator system consists of a nine-foot compound knotted leader with about five feet of fluorescent red mono in the butt. (These formulas are shown in Chapter 2.) I

Early in the season, trout feed heavily on nymphs such as this stonefly nymph.

install two small tube-type indicators on these leaders. (I especially like those made by Scientific Anglers.) I place one of these about three feet above my nymph, and the second one about three feet further up the leader.

There are many types of indicators available and I'd suggest experimenting to find the one which you like best.

When fishing, try to watch the indicator that is closest to the nymph, looking for the slightest hesitation when the trout takes it. If my fly is so deep that I cannot see the bottom indicator, I watch the upper indicator. If I cannot see this, I watch the fluorescent red mono in the butt of the leader. The instant I see a strike, I quickly set the hook.

The mid-pool area we discussed in Chapter 5 is the ideal area to fish nymphs early in the season. Trout hold on the stream bottom here where the large stones give them protection from the current. As the stream warms slightly, deep areas along the edges of incoming riffles (at the head of pools) are good areas to fish with nymphs because this is another place where trout can find protection. Hiding near the bottom, this location also allows them to gain access to many other naturals.

EARLY-SEASON DRY-FLY FISHING ON SMALL STREAMS

Many anglers are so fond of fishing dry flies that they use them early in the season even if the streams are cool and a little higher than some anglers consider ideal.

The back eddies discussed in Chapter 5 frequently attract surface-feeding trout when streams are slightly high. The reduced flows and shallow water here enable trout to feed easily on natural foods on the surface. These are my favorite early season feeding stations, and I always pause and study them carefully to see if

The Mr. Rapidan Parachute dry fly is an excellent fly to use early in the season. It floats exceptionally well on choppy current, it's easy for the angler to see and it closely matches several important early-season insects.

I can spot any trout holding here before making a cast. Once I spot a trout, I move in closely, without scaring them, and drift my dry fly directly to one.

The corner is the easiest feeding station from which to catch a large trout on a dry fly early in the season. Even if the main flow of the stream is racing by several feet away the trout hold in the protection of the large upstream boulder and feed without expending much energy.

These corners are easy to fish if you keep in mind that the trout always face into the current. This means that in these spots

Large trout often hold in the protected corners of pools, just inches from the racing currents, and feed actively on insects drifting on the surface of the stream.

they will be facing toward the bank, away from the main portion of the stream.

To fish the corner I wade in from below it, or from the main part of the stream, depending upon the depth of the stream, and cast my dry fly about a foot out in front of the feeding station. Since there are many fast currents swirling around this dinner-plate-size feeding station, it is important to extend your fly rod up and out far enough to bridge these fast currents and get a natural drift over the trout.

FISHING MEDIUM-SIZE STREAMS EARLY IN THE SEASON

Medium-size streams can provide good fishing early in the season, once one learns how to master full water levels which are normally encounterd at this time.

One can achieve the best fly presentation in larger streams by carefully evaluating the area that you plan to fish, wading to a location which will enable you to be in complete control. In addition to the area you plan to fish, you need to evaluate the currents between your position and those locations. For example, if a stretch around some large boulders 3/4 of the way across the stream looks good, and the current between you and that area is fast and choppy, you may want to wade across the stream at a gentle area, fishing that stretch from the far side of the stream. This is a much more effective way to fish in a stream of this size during the spring rather than by attempting to make exceptionally long casts over mixed currents. Rolling currents can rob you of the depth you need for your underwater flies, or cause your dry flies to drag, thus robbing you of natural presentations. On the lower West Gallatin River in Montana, I often recross the stream many times each day to fish it effectively.

On medium-size streams it is very important to accurately evaluate potential feeding stations in order to position yourself properly to gain control presentation and drift of your fly.

EARLY-SEASON NYMPHING ON MEDIUM-SIZE STREAMS

The same upstream dead-drifting tactics used on smaller headwater streams are effective on these streams. If they are shallow enough to allow us to wade into the similar areas in order to make almost straight upstream presentations, fishing can be successful.

In many streams, this is extremely effective just below incoming riffles. By wading upstream and fishing the interface—where fast water meets slow water—one can get great nymph fishing early in the season.

Frequently, deep riffles in the middle of pools on many of these streams are much too deep to wade in the spring. This prevents us from being able to fish them with upstream dead-drifting methods.

Large rainbow trout often take nymphs fished along the stream bottom with a dead-drifting technique.

However, a technique the late Charlie Brooks taught me is extremely effective in deep portions of a pool. Brooks used the method in very large rivers with some custom-made fast-sinking fly lines and we named it the Brooks Method. But since we're discussing smaller streams, where a floating line will work fine, we'll make a few minor changes and call this swing nymphing.

Swing nymphing will enable you to get your nymphs deeper than any technique you can use with a floating line, and it's easy to learn. In fact, many beginning students in my flyfishing workshops take some of their best fish with this method. Sometimes, they do so on their first day!

This method is completely different from upstream dead-drift nymphing because there we are wading upstream, casting upstream, and detecting strikes by looking for them on our indicator system. In swing nymphing, we are wading downstream, casting upstream, and detecting the strikes by feeling them.

Use this method on medium-size trout streams—ones that are large enough to enable you to wade downstream without scaring trout. Wade down the side of the pool to a spot located near the side of the stream where the deep part of the pool begins. Your first cast should be about 15 feet long, up and across the stream at a 45° angle. Allow the nymph to sink deeply, then extend your rod up and out over the stream at a 45° angle while simultaneously taking up slack. Swing the rod downstream (in the shape of an arc), at the same speed that the nymph is drifting. This swinging phase is critical because if you swing your fly rod too slowly, slack will develop in your line or leader and you will not be able to feel strikes. If you swing it too fast, you may pull the nymph so far off the bottom of the stream that trout will not be able to see it.

Swing Nymphing

This technique is very effective in deep pools and pockets which are too deep to wade.

Step 1: The nymph is cast up and across stream at about a 45-degree angle about five feet upstream of the deep area you plan to fish.

Step 2: The nymph is allowed to sink deeply on a slack line. When the nymph has drifted down and is straight out from you, the slack line is pulled in with the line hand. Use care not to lift the nymph up very far from the stream bottom.

Step 3: From this point to about 45 degrees downstream, your nymph will be drifting right along the stream bottom. The instant you feel the trout's strike, set the hook quickly.

The swing-nymphing technique is an excellent way to fish a nymph along the bottom in the fast, deep runs of a medium-size streams.

Trout strikes may feel like bumps or rubs. The instant you feel these tugs, set the hook quickly with an up-sweeping rod motion.

If you don't get a strike, stand in the same position and make your next cast several feet further up and out, and repeat the same line-handling technique. Continue this with successive casts until you've covered all of the water out to about 30 feet. Then wade about ten feet downstream, and repeat the process. By continuing this all the way down, beside the deep parts of pools, you'll give every trout a chance to see your nymph.

EARLY-SEASON STREAMER FISHING ON MEDIUM-SIZE STREAMS

Streamers which imitate minnows are effective on medium-size streams after spring run-off has started early in the season.

Large brown trout often feed aggressively early in the season and can be caught on streamers.

However, full streams restrict the areas where we can expect good fishing. For example, the deep and fast mid-pool sections of these streams may still be flowing so quickly that it is very difficult to get streamers to the bottom. When this occurs, you cannot fish effectively. Following, though, are the three best areas to fish with streamers when streams are full during springtime.

Just below riffles, there are usually protected areas which stretch from the bank and then out for about 30 feet. Staying close to the bank, cast a streamer (such as a black Woolly Bugger) across the stream and allow it to sink deeply. Then, using a slow retrieve, strip the fly about six inches every ten seconds. Wade slowly downstream about 20 feet, repeating this pattern about every five feet. Usually, I take some nice trout this way. (A)

The second area to fish with streamers are the protected cuts among large boulders located within 30 feet of the bank.

Use the same tactics here that you would use below the riffle at the head of pools, except that here, you may have to allow more time for your streamer to sink deeply before you begin the retrieve. (B)

The tail of the pool is the third area to explore with your streamer in large pools early in the season. Often there will be a 20- to 30-foot-wide stretch of river running parallel to the bank (in the last 50 feet of the pool), where trout can find protection from strong currents to feed on minnows.

Stay well away from the water you plan to fish, frequently staying along the bank. The same streamers and tactics used in other parts of the pool are effective here as well. (C)

EARLY-SEASON DRY-FLY FISHING ON MEDIUM-SIZE STREAMS

There are times when you can find good dry fly-fishing on medium-size streams early in the season. As mentioned earlier, when evaluating the needs of trout, there is an interplay between water temperature and water level which dictates the feeding habits of trout. If the water temperature is quite low (below 40° F) or the stream is unusually high, trout may not be willing to feed on the surface. However, let me tell you about a situation that I encountered in the Gorge section of the West Branch of the Ausable River in New York's Adirondac Mountains.

I had never fished the stream before, and although it was carrying a lot of water, I thought I could wade some areas if I was careful. I took the water temperature, and it read 49° F. And although that temperature was still cool, it prompted me to start with dry flies.

A size 14 Royal Wulff seemed to be the fly the rainbows had been waiting for all winter. That day I took many nice

Selection of the correct dry fly improves their chances to catch trout early in the season. Good floating qualities and high angler visibilty are extremely important.

trout by wading up the side of the river, drifting my fly within two to three feet of the bank ahead of me. Even the protected areas close to the banks below the riffles gave me several nice trout.

I didn't realize, though, I had violated local protocol until I came out of the stream to talk to an angler who had been watching me catch the rainbows. He said he'd been fishing the stream for many years but that he had no idea trout would rise to drys this early in the season. I suppose that in this case, my inexperience on the stream actually worked to my advantage.

If you would like to fish these streams with dry flies early in season, seek out areas where trout can find protection from the current. The areas along banks are always good possibilities, and if you can locate back eddies, either along the banks or behind large boulders, you can get good fishing.

FISHING HIGH-MEADOW STREAMS EARLY IN THE SEASON

The quality of fishing, and when it begins on these streams, depends greatly upon their latitude and altitude. Some provide good fishing before the spring run-off, but most don't have good fishing until afterwards.

Nymphs and small streamers—fished in the areas behind boulders and the slower areas along the banks, especially the undercut areas—will give you the best fishing.

On selected streams, heavy hatches of large stoneflies can bring good dry-fly fishing. This often surprises anglers new to this sport, though, because in many cases you can only see about two feet down into the streams.

Anglers who are willing to experiment, staying observant early in the season, often find great action.

LATE-SPRING AND SUMMER TACTICS

In this chapter, we'll start by covering the time period when streams drop to manageable levels, and when water temperatures become warm enough for trout to feed actively.

This period varies greatly depending upon the part of the country you're fishing. For example, if you're fishing the Blue Ridge Mountains in Virginia, this may begin in early April, but if you're fishing some of the higher streams in the northern Rockies, this may not take place until June.

HEADWATER STREAMS

As streams grow warmer, beginning to drop, they begin to offer the type of trout fishing which many anglers consider the finest of the whole season.

Aquatic insect hatches now occur in full swing, and trout feed actively upon them. During the period when the emergence of naturals is most frequent, trout often hold in protected feeding stations, taking dry flies as they are drifted overhead.

Since most anglers prefer to catch their fish on dry flies under these conditions, let's look at these tactics.

Even with full streams, during this time of the year, trout in small streams are wary enough to compel us to fish upstream for them. As you approach a pool from below, pause for a few minutes in order to evaluate the whole pool before you. First, try to locate feeding stations which trout might select so that they can feed efficiently. Since they must be able to gain enough food

The emergence of many insects and blooming of wildflowers often coincide. When this jack-in-the-pulpit blooms in the mid-Atlantic area, several important mayfly hatches are in full swing.

Trout feed heavily on mayflies and often select feeding stations close to the main currents which carry the insects.

value from what they eat, the amount of energy that they use to capture it must be of equal value. This tells you that they will take advantage of feeding stations which are close to main currents because this is where natural insects drift through the pool. However, trout need something to block the full force of currents from their bodies—otherwise they would swim themselves to death. In headwater streams they often take advantage of boulders, gravel bars and even reverse currents to block the full force of the current from their bodies. Several of the feeding stations we discussed in Chapter 5 provide this kind of protection in a full stream.

The second thing you need to determine as you stand below the pool is where you must present your fly in order to get a natural drag-free drift over these feeding stations.

The final, and most important, information you must discern is how to approach the pool. You must select a casting position that will enable you to accurately deliver your fly to the target, controlling the drift to prevent drag, and you must move into this position without scaring the trout.

Since the lip is the first feeding station you'll come to, let's look at an effective way to fish it. Most lips in these pools are formed as a large boulder or several bushel—basket-size boulders momentarily dam the flow of the water before it leaves a pool. Trout often hold just inches upstream of this boulder in the protected buffer which it provides from the current.

Placing your fly onto the current that will drift it naturally is essential to fooling trout.

Since there are a fair number of insects on the water here, always observe this area closely for a minute or two in order to see if there are any rising trout hiding in the depths. If you see a rise-form, you know precisely where to drift your fly. If you don't see a feeder, cast your fly about two feet above the boulder, letting the current drift it to where other trout may be resting.

It is extremely important that after you make your presentation cast you hold the fly-rod high at about a 45-degree angle out over the stream in order to bridge the fast water racing out of the pool in the lower part of the lip. If your fly line or leader falls into this fast current, it will cause the fly to race along the surface in an unnatural way and trout will not take it. In fact, I have seen flies dragged in this manner which have actually scared trout, making them dash up into the pool.

If you don't get a strike on the first drift over the lip, experiment with casts several feet to the right, and left, and maybe five-feet further up into the pool, in case you've misread where you thought trout would be. However, this is seldom necessary. After you gain experience on these mountain streams, you'll be able to anticipate trouts' precise lip-feeding stations within less than a foot. This will probably become the most dependable location within the pool to catch a trout on a dry fly. The only reasons for not catching a trout here, when the stream conditions are favorable, is that you spooked him with your approach, or that you got unnatural drag with your fly as you drifted it over him.

As you fish up the pool, the tail of the pool now becomes a valuable feeding station to fish with your dry flies. This is especially true if there are a fair number of natural insects on the stream and the trout are rising to them. Anticipating precisely where trout will hold, if you don't see a rising trout on the tail of the pool because there are seldom prominent features which give trout protection from the current. They usually seek out

Trout hold in the tails of pools where they can sip the naturals from the surface. Fishing to these feeding trout is one of the most enjoyable aspects of angling.

slight depressions in the stream bottom to hold in, waiting there for insects to drift by them.

For this reason, fish the tail of the pool with about six casts, spaced every several feet, from left to right. This will enable trout to see your fly wherever they're holding.

It is extremely important to keep in mind that you should strive to make the first cast to each feeding station as close to perfect as possible. When this is achieved, you usually get your trout on the first drift. Remember, these trout do not have an overabundance of natural insects to feed upon so they have learned to take them as soon as they drift into view. Otherwise, if the insect continues to drift downstream, they never get a second shot at him. Don't forget, make your first cast your best cast!

A rewarding fringe benefit of fishing the mountain streams is being in the midst of the magnificent wildflowers.

The back eddies and corners discussed earlier are valuable areas to fish when streams are dropping and warming up. The tactics are the same as those which we covered earlier in this book.

Heads of pools are well worth exploring when water levels drop. Many of the best trout hold along the sides of the heavy current which comes down through the head of the pool. Think in terms of drifting your flies where the fast water coming down the center meets the slow water on the sides of the flow. You may not know precisely where the trout will hold up and down this flow, but you can estimate quite accurately where they will be from side to side.

I like to fish the head of the pool by making about six casts on each side of the center flow, each one being several

Nymphs fished along the stream bottom in the deep parts of pools often give anglers many trout.

feet further upstream than the previous cast. In this way, I drift my flies over all of the holding trout.

Many anglers who enjoy fishing nymphs at this time of the year find that they make some of their best catches in deep mid—pool areas in large pools.

The head of the pool should also be explored with nymphs. As I just mentioned, when fishing these areas with dry flies, the best action usually comes from the sides of the main flow along that interface where the fast water meets the slow water on the sides. The same areas are productive with nymphs.

Dead-drifting and swing-nymphing tactics are effective in these areas. But, I'd suggest using the method which will enable you to fish your nymphs deeply, while still being able to quickly detect strikes.

MEDIUM-SIZE STREAMS

As spring turns into summer, many of these larger streams provide outstanding fishing. Plan your overnight trips to take advantage of the hatches of aquatic insects which occur at this time.

If you prefer a technical approach, you can check the hatch charts in Chapter 4. However, if you like a more hands-on approach, you can wait until you get to the stream to see what's hatching then match those insects with the flies in your fly box. I use a combination of these two methods whenever I fish in new areas.

Drys, nymphs, and streamers are all effective in large streams at this time of the year. Yet, some anglers have a stronger preference for one of these methods over the another, and that is fine depending upon how you like to fish. Personally, I've found that I get my best fishing by using all three methods, especially when I fine-tune them to existing stream conditions. Let's see how this works.

Medium-size streams can be intimidating but if you break them down into the areas observed in headwater streams and apply the same angling tactics, they can be easily mastered.

A good example was the day when I drove about ten hours to the West Branch of the Saranac River which is one of my favorite trout streams in northern New York. As I parked the camper beside the stream late in the afternoon, I was pleased to see there were many March Brown mayflies hatching, and that there were a number of trout feeding on the surface. I put on a size 14 March Brown dry fly and had great fishing until dark.

The next morning, I started with the same dry fly, but I didn't get a strike during the first hour. There were no emerging mayflies, and no rising trout, so the dry fly had been a poor choice.

I replaced my dry fly with a size 12 March Brown Nymph and began fishing it dead-drifted upstream. I concentrated on the shallows to the sides of the riffles, as well as to the sloping gravel bars along the banks, because many of the March Brown Nymphs

Small feeder brooks that enter large streams often improve insect hatches and water temperatures, trout feed more actively thus increasing the quality of the fishing.

make a mini-migration to these areas prior to emergence. This worked quite well and I caught many nice trout.

Just by chance, my fishing partner William Downey was about 100 yards downstream. Seeing no rising trout, he started with a streamer, fishing the fast runs below the riffles. This turned out to be a wise choice because he caught the largest brown trout of his life!

Let's look at some of the tactics which are effective with drys, nymphs, and streamers at this time of the year on medium-size streams.

DRY FLIES

The obvious moment of when to go to dry flies at this time of the year is when you see trout rising to feed on specific aquatic insect hatches. There are many hatches where the duns are quite heavy. They emerge first, from mid afternoon until dusk, and then the spinners are on the water during the last hour of daylight. However, there are exceptions to this axiom, such as the Pale Morning Dun, so you should be observant of what is happening on the stream and make the necessary adjustments.

Even when there is no concentrated hatch, I've often done well at this time of the year by fishing the water with high-floating flies that have fish-appeal. Good examples include: Royal Wulffs, Light Humpies, and Mr. Rapidans. The sections of the stream to fish are the edges of incoming riffles, around boulders, and along undercut banks.

Streams which run through open fields often provide good surface fishing during the summer with grasshopper and cricket patterns. Obviously, these are most effective, though, when fished along banks where trout are accustomed to seeing the real insect. These insects are often blown from the fields, and land on the water with a splat, so this is the way I present my

There are many great medium-size trout streams throughout the Rocky Mountains where one can find good fly-fishing with nymphs and drys.

flies when a more gentle, natural presentation fails to bring strikes.

If you come to an undercut bank that has an old log in it, take extra time to fish this carefully with a big hopper such as a size 10 Dave's Hopper. Big browns often hold in these areas, and by showing them a big mouthful, it may be more than they can resist.

If your stream has large trees along the banks with limbs reaching out over the stream, trout which live there probably feed heavily upon natural ants and beetles that fall into the stream.

For example, one of the streams I frequently fish has an almost solid canopy of trees which stretches for several hundred yards. Most of the time, I can find many trout feeding on natural ants and beetles and they will take my size 16 Black Fur Ants and size 16 Murray's Flying Beetles the instant they see them.

NYMPHS

Technically, nymph, larva, and pupa flies match the underwater forms of various aquatic insects, and I'm confident that many trout take them because they look like these naturals. However, I also believe that many trout that we catch on nymphs take them because they simply look like something good to eat.

Sometimes, the rougher our nymphs look, the more trout we are able to catch with them. A very special friend of mine, the late Charlie Brooks of West Yellowstone, Montana, was one of the finest nymph fishermen in the country. Since he was also an investigator and skilled fly designer, he understood a lot about imitating naturals. Charlie's personal ties looked rather crude but buggy, a fact which he took pride in because all of them were very effective in catching large trout. A fishing friend of Brooks one day said, "Charlie, your nymphs are outstanding, but if I throw them on the

The Bechler River in Yellowstone National Park is an excellent medium-size trout stream where anglers catch large trout on large nymphs.

ground and stomp on them, they take even more trout." Naturally, he was kidding, but the point he was making was that often the rougher nymphs seem to fool trout best.

The same tactics we use to fish nymphs in these streams early in the season (see Chapter 7) are effective at this juncture in time as well. However, keep in mind that streams are dropping and that you may need a more cautious approach to fool the largest fish.

Use the upstream dead-drifting method at this time of year for just this reason. The corners below the riffles, and the shallow portions of the riffles, just before they dump into the main parts of pools, are great areas to fish with mayfly nymphs and caddis larvae if there is a cobblestone bottom. If there are a number of basketball-size stones here, this is the habitat for natural, large stonefly nymphs. Use a size 8 Brooks Dark Stonefly Nymph.

There is no wrong time to fish nymphs in medium-size streams at this time of the year. However, if you hit a point when you discover high or discolored water, nymphs are definitely a good choice.

STREAMERS

Streamers are often considered searching patterns at this time of the year. You go to them when you want to cover a lot of water in a hurry.

Some anglers like to fish streamers because they feel these larger flies will attract larger trout. Actually, there is some merit to this, and I've found myself following this logic from time to time. Some of the richest medium-size streams hold many more large trout than some anglers realize because when they fish their dry flies and small nymphs, they don't catch as many large trout as they would like. Try going to these

Many anglers like to fish streamers on medium-size streams because they know they can catch some of the largest trout on these flies.

same streams at dusk and fish your streamers deeply, under the undercut banks and down falls, and you may be surprised by what you catch.

HIGH-MEADOW STREAMS

Many of these streams are best fished from late spring through the summer, but the six weeks after the spring run-off are often considered the best period.

While the streams are still a little high and slightly discolored, anglers get their best fishing with nymphs and streamers, using the tactics we've just covered. However, as hatches of

*Many high-meadow streams become low late
in summer and trout become wary
requiring that we use a very cautious approach.*

aquatic insects begin to occur, anglers like to switch over to dry flies because these work better under these conditions.

The diverse bottom composition, nature of streams, and gradient, all influence specific aquatic insect hatches you may encounter. After you've fished a specific stream for several years, though, you'll be able to predict hatches with great accuracy. However, when fishing a stream for the first time, a sound tactic is to be observant of the flies which are hatching, then match these with your dry flies.

Terrestrial insects become an important part of the trout diet during the summer on many of these streams, and anglers make good catches with patterns that are able to match them.

If you don't see rising trout, use a pattern such as a size 12 Dave's Hopper to fish all of the likely-looking feeding areas. Undercut banks, and the edges of incoming riffles in the heads of pools, will often provide you with several nice trout.

Occasionally, I'll see a trout swing out from under a bank and pull up under my Hopper only to refuse it. Successive drifts with the Hopper also fail to bring a strike. Knowing precisely where the trout is, though, can be a big help even if he won't take the Hopper. Frequently, I can take these trout by going to a finer leader, drifting a size 16 Black Fur Ant or a size 16 Murray's Flying Beetle over them.

In fact, I've taken many trout in streams on ants and beetle patterns which I'd seen rising just before to small insects which I couldn't identify. I believe there are so many natural ants and beetles around these streams that, no matter what, trout are often willing to take them.

Terrestrial flies, such as the Murray's Flying Beetle and the Mr. Rapidan Ant, are very productive on high-meadow streams during summer and fall.

Chapter 9

THE FABULOUS FALL

SMALL STREAMS

Fall is a wonderful time to be on trout streams, because not only is the foliage magnificent, but trout fishing may be better than it is at any other time of year.

Cool nights cause water temperatures to drop from the stress-inducing levels found on many streams during August, thus, prompting trout to feed actively. In addition, if there are brook trout or browns in your stream, nature is telling them to increase their feeding in preparation for their fall spawning.

The author enjoys fishing mountain streams in the fall because trout feed well on the surface.

Another seasonal feature which helps trout is that there is a good supply of natural insects on the stream. Terrestrial insects, which were so important to trout in the summer, are still present on many streams, and there are good-size hatches of Diptera midges, with richer streams having large numbers of *Beatis* mayflies.

These factors—ideal water temperatures, the necessity to feed for good health during the spawning season, and the relative abundance of food—prompt trouts' desire to feed. However, an important physical factor can alter their manner of feeding in small streams and you must adapt to this in order to make consistently good catches in the fall.

I'm referring to the low water levels anglers encounter on headwater streams early in the fall. On some of the best streams, the volume of water pushing through the pools is not great enough to deliver natural insects to trout as quickly as they want them. Trout, therefore, adopt a cruising method of feeding. That's right, they actually go out and search for natural insects.

Fishing for cruisers just might be my favorite way to fish for trout. Admittedly, it can be challenging, even frustrating, but mastering these one-on-one contests with tough trout can be very gratifying.

THERE ARE TWO BASIC WAYS TO FISH FOR CRUISERS

One method is to begin by watching a trout's rise form as they sip in naturals from the surface of the stream. Then, based on this path, try to anticipate which way they will head, casting your fly out in front of them, hoping that they'll see it and take it. If, however, the fish changes directions, it might not see it. You may get a second shot at the trout if you wait until it is well away from

Fishing dry flies to trout you can see cruising just beneath the stream's surface is a very exciting technique for low, clear streams in the fall.

your fly, then carefully pick the fly up, and cast it out in front of the fish again.

The method I prefer to use when I see a trout cruising is to carefully move in close enough to see the trout. Once I'm in position, I allow it to take a few natural insects. This enables me to confirm that I have not scared the fish with my approach, and it helps me to know precisely where it is, and in which direction the fish is feeding. Now, I can cast my fly accurately out in front of the trout, with good expectations of taking it.

These cruisers are seldom selective, but realizing that they have been feeding predominately on terrestrial insects for the past several months, and that there are still many terrestrials around the streams, show them a Murray's Flying Beetle size 16. Most trout will take this fly as soon as they see it.

Some areas get rains in the fall that bring streams up enough to provide excellent dry-fly fishing throughout the stream. By fishing the best-looking feeding stations with high-floating dry flies, such as a Royal Wulff or Mr. Rapidan, you can have fast action. This can be equally successful on both small and medium-size streams.

Depending upon the latitude and altitude of the stream, you can go underwater with nymphs and streamers and get good fishing until October or November.

Dead-drifting and swing-nymphing tactics we already discussed for useage during the spring fishing season are both effective techniques to use during the fall as well.

MEDIUM-SIZE STREAMS

In medium-size streams I've had good fishing with streamers in the northern Rockies well into October. I don't catch as many trout as I did a month earlier, but I catch many more large trout. Further south, I've had successful streamer fishing throughout the country, through November.

An effective streamer tactic in larger streams late in the season is to wade down the side of the river, casting across the stream. After the streamer is close to the bottom of the stream, use a very slow line hand stripping action that pulls the streamer about six inches every ten seconds. Frequently, the hot spot will be in the deepest part of the pool so I like to cover this thoroughly.

I like to fish these streamers on floating fly lines, but in some cases, if pools are quite deep or unusually fast, I go to a fast, sinking-tip fly line, and a six-foot leader. If I'm not catching trout or bumping the bottom with my flies, occasionally I assume trout are not seeing my offerings. This is my cue to switch to the sinking-tip line. It is amazing how often this simple ploy enables me to catch some nice trout that I couldn't take with my floating line.

You can catch many trout in medium-size streams in the fall by fishing streamers very slowly across the bottom of the stream.

Index

Adirondac Mountains	77
Ausable River, West Branch	77
backing	14
Beaver Dam	60
Bechler River	49, 93
Big Stoney Creek	49
Blue Ridge Mountains	58, 80
brook trout	11, 55, 58
Brooks, Charlie	72, 93
brown trout	75, 51, 58, 59
caddisflies	36, 46
cutthroat trout	52, 54, 58
Dave's Hopper	38, 40, 42
Downey, William	91
dry flies	80, 91
emergency pack	19
feeding stations	43, 44, 45
Firehole River	59
fly boxes	17
fly casting	29, 30, 31, 32
fly-fishing schools	29
fly line	13, 14
fly reel	13
fly rod	12, 13
fly selections	40, 41, 42
gadgets	17, 18, 19
hatch charts	35
hats	16, 17
Hewitt, Ed	8
high-meadow streams	52, 53, 54
improved clinch knot	25, 26
knots	19, 20, 21, 22
leader formulas	27
leaders	14
Madison River	58
mayflies	33, 46
minnows	39
Montana	49, 59
Mr. Rapidan Dry Fly	34, 91
Mr. Rapidan Parachute	40, 67
Mr. Rapidan Ant	38, 97
Murray's Flying Beetle	38, 40, 92, 97, 100
Murray's Strymph	39, 40, 41
nail knot	22, 23
needle knot	23, 24
New York	49, 77, 89
Oconaluftee River	49
Penns Creek	49
Pennsylvania	49
Rainbow Trout	58
raincoat	15
reading the water	43, 45
schools	29, 72
sculpin	39
spotting trout	55
Shenandoah Valley	49
Shenk's Cricket	40
Shenk's Hopper	38
Shenk's Sculpin	39, 40
Shenk's White Streamer	39
Smokies	49
stoneflies	35, 46, 65
sunglasses	17
surgeon's knot	24, 25
swing nymphing	72
terrestrial insects	37, 38
vest	14, 15
Virginia	49, 58, 80
waders	15, 16
Waterman, Charley	59, 60
West Branch of the Saranac River	49, 89
West Gallatin River	48, 49
Whitlock's Sculpin	39, 41
Yellowstone National Park	48, 49, 54, 93

Also Available from Frank Amato Publications

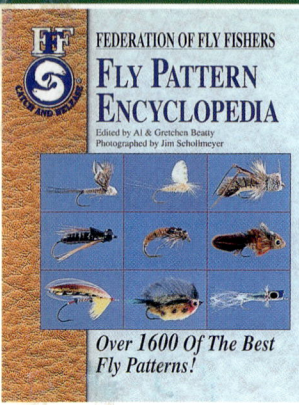

FEDERATION OF FLY-FISHERS FLY PATTERN ENCYCLOPEDIA
Over 1600 of the Best Fly Patterns
SB: $39.95   ISBN: 1-57188-208-1

DRY-FLY PATTERNS FOR THE NEW MILLENNIUM
SB: $19.95   ISBN: 1-57188-244-8
HB: $29.95   ISBN: 1-57188-245-6

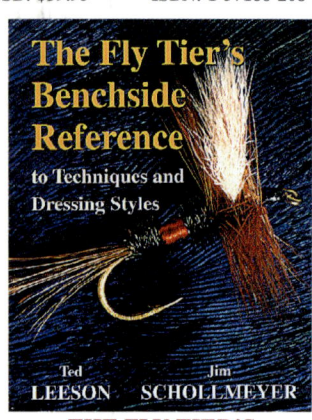
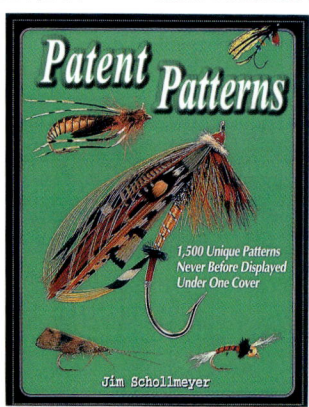

THE FLY TIER'S BENCHSIDE REFERENCE
HB: $100.00   ISBN: 1-57188-126-3
CD: $59.95 For PC or Mac   ISBN: 1-57188-259-6

PATENT PATTERNS
SB: $29.95   ISBN: 1-57188-279-0
Spiral HB: $39.95   ISBN: 1-57188-280-4

To Order call 1-800-541-9498, or go to www.amatobooks.com